Ravenscourt
B·O·O·K·S

Once There Were Two

By

Carole Gerber

SRA

Columbus, OH

Photos: Cover, ©Baseball Hall of Fame Library, Cooperstown, N.Y.; **4, 19,** ©Baseball Hall of Fame Library, Cooperstown, N.Y.; **26,** ©Ernie Sisto/New York Times; **40,** ©Bettman/Corbis; **43,** ©Baseball Hall of Fame Library, Cooperstown, N.Y.

SRAonline.com

 SRA

Send all inquiries to this address:
SRA/McGraw-Hill
4400 Easton Commons
Columbus, OH 43219

Printed in the United States of America.

ISBN: 978-0-07-612185-4
MHID: 0-07-612185-2

4 5 6 7 8 9 MAL 13 12 11 10 09

The **McGraw·Hill** Companies

Contents

——— Chapter 1 ———

Unknown Sports Heroes

It was a perfect day for the last baseball game of the 1936 season. The sky was blue. The afternoon air was warm. The crowd was happy.

A soft breeze blew through the stands. It fluttered the hems of skirts. It flapped the ends of collars. It cooled the fans' bodies, but it did not cool their excitement. They roared when their favorite player stepped up to the batter's box.

The man was a catcher. He spent much of his time crouched behind home plate, so it was always a pleasure to see him standing. At six feet one inch tall and 205 pounds, he was one of the biggest players on the team.

*His right sleeve was rolled above his muscular forearm. The brim of his cap was pushed back. His large body looked relaxed.

But the fans weren't fooled. They could read the look on his face. It sent them a clear message: "I'm going to do it again."

"It" was hitting a home run. The fans wished for it as much as the man did. *Whack!* They got their wish sooner than they expected.

The batter hit the first pitch high toward center field. It cleared the fence and sailed right out of the park. The fans went wild. They yelled. They jumped. They hugged. Some threw their hats in the air.

Any home run would be cause for joy. But this one was special. It was the 84th home run* the man had hit that season.

Who was this amazing player? What team was he on? Was it Babe Ruth playing for the New York Yankees?

No! Ruth had already set a record. He had led the American League in home runs in 1927. He had hit 60 homers that season.

The batter was Josh Gibson of the Pittsburgh Crawfords. Nine years after Ruth set the record, Gibson broke it. He slugged 24 more home runs than Ruth. Gibson was called "the black Babe Ruth." At the time, no one thought to call Ruth "the white Josh Gibson." Maybe they should have.

Gibson was one of the most powerful batters in baseball. He was the only player ever to hit two home runs out of the park at Griffith Stadium in Washington, D.C.

Josh Gibson, playing for the Homestead Grays,
trots home after hitting a home run in Griffith Stadium

Gibson was also a fine catcher. He could run fast. And he set four batting records. Yet few fans today know about this great ballplayer. Why? Because he didn't play on a major league team.

Instead, Gibson played on one of the dozens of Negro League teams, as did many other talented African Americans. Because of this, many baseball fans have never heard of them.

Gibson wasn't the only great player on his team. He had many outstanding teammates. Many baseball experts say the 1936 Pittsburgh Crawfords was the best team ever.

Oscar Charleston was also on the 1936 Pittsburgh Crawfords. Many people believe he was the best all-around player in Negro League history. Fans knew Jimmie Crutchfield as an excellent batter and outfielder. Third baseman William Julius "Judy" Johnson was known for his game-winning hits. Another teammate, James "Cool Papa" Bell, was the fastest man in baseball. But the Crawfords' most famous player was Leroy "Satchel" Paige. He is considered one of the greatest pitchers of all time.

From 1920 to 1955, hundreds of talented African American ballplayers joined the Negro Leagues. These players would have welcomed the chance to play in the major leagues. Why? The pay there was much higher. The fame was greater. And the players got more respect.

Only one thing kept these players in the Negro Leagues. It was simply that many Caucasian owners of major league teams did not want African American players on their teams. What could African American players do about the segregation rules? They loved the game, so they formed their own leagues.

Huge crowds of African American fans turned out for their games. They dressed in their best clothes. Attending Negro League games was the popular thing to do.

Many Caucasian fans also came to the games. They admired the African American players. They cheered and clapped for the players, but they sat apart from the African American fans.

Once there were two sets of leagues—one for Caucasian players and one for African American players. Most people saw nothing wrong with separate teams and separate seats. They just believed it was the way things were.

— Chapter 2 —

Play Ball!

"You're out!" These simple words were first shouted in 1825 in Hamden, New Jersey. That's where some people think the first baseball game was played. The sport quickly caught on.

Baseball clubs sprang up in the 1830s in New York City and Philadelphia, Pennsylvania. At first, each club had its own rules. Baseball as we know it was not played until 1845 by the New York Knickerbockers.

Right from the start, people loved this "modern" game of baseball. Baseball clubs were formed throughout the Northeast. Men who served in the U.S. Civil War learned the game and took it home. That's how baseball spread across the United States.

Soldiers from the Midwest learned to play baseball when they trained at Union army camps in the East. The war also helped baseball spread to the South. Union soldiers held in Southern prison camps played baseball. Confederate soldiers watched them and learned the rules.

News about this exciting game soon spread beyond the army. In 1861 two African American teams played one another in Brooklyn, New York. In 1869 an all-black team from Philadelphia played against an all-white team and won. Even so, the National Association of Baseball Players would not admit the African American team to their league.

During the following years a few dozen African American men played on Caucasian teams. The first to do so was a pitcher named John W. "Bud" Fowler. In 1878 he joined a minor league Caucasian team called the Live Oaks.

Some of the Caucasian players did not want an African American on their team. They found ways to "accidentally" stick their spiked shoes into his legs. But Fowler did not let them run him off the team. Instead, he invented the first shin guards! He taped pieces of wood to his legs so the spikes could not hurt him.

In 1883 an African American catcher named Moses Fleetwood "Fleet" Walker joined a Caucasian minor league team called the Toledo Blue Stockings.

The team was set to play the Chicago White Stockings. The other team's coach, Adrian Constantine, objected. Constantine, nicknamed Cap Anson, did not want his team to play against an African American player.

The Toledo team's coach did not care. He put Walker in the game. Cap Anson was upset. He let the game go on, but he held a grudge.

The Blue Stockings kept Walker on the team in 1884 when they joined the major leagues. He was the first African American player in the major leagues. Walker played in 42 games that year. Then he was injured, and his contract was not renewed. So he joined a Caucasian minor league team in Jersey City, New Jersey.

In 1887 Cap Anson's team came up against Jersey City. Cap Anson refused to let his team on the field if Walker and another African American teammate played. This time he got his way. Walker and the other African American player, George Stovey, were taken out of the game.

Both men were outstanding players. Stovey was the team's top pitcher. He was so good that John Ward wanted to sign him. Ward owned a major league team in New York.

This would have been Stovey's big break. But Cap Anson complained again. He was a powerful man. So Ward backed down. Stovey began playing in the Negro Leagues instead. The pay was low, but it was the only place he could get a job playing baseball.

*Walker played for two more years in the minor leagues. Then he left baseball and founded a newspaper for African Americans.

In the meantime, Anson continued to use his power to keep African Americans off major league teams. John McGraw was the manager of the New York Giants. In the early 1900s he tried a trick to get around Cap Anson. McGraw signed a player whose name, he claimed, was "Chief Tokahoma." He said the player was a Native American.

The player was really an African American man named Charlie Grant. When Cap Anson found out, he forced McGraw to fire Grant.

No one knows why Cap Anson had the beliefs he did. He had played baseball before becoming a coach. He loved the game. He worked hard to make* it popular.

A more sensible man would have recruited the best players, whatever their race. But Cap Anson was not sensible. He also had a bad temper. His cruelty showed in a number of ways. He screamed at his Caucasian players. Sometimes he hit them.

In spite of this, he had a big influence over other team owners. He made them afraid to recruit African American players. Sadly, Cap Anson's prejudice lived on in the actions of others he had influenced, even after he died.

It was not until 1947—25 years after Cap Anson's death—that an African American man played for a major league team again. His name was Jackie Robinson.

— **Chapter 3** —

Building Communities

In Cap Anson's day, segregation was not confined to sports. Many Caucasians—and some African Americans—felt the two races should be kept separate in every way.

In southern states, "Jim Crow" laws were passed. The term "Jim Crow" came from an African American character played by Caucasian actors in traveling shows. The laws took away many rights that African Americans had been granted after the U.S. Civil War. The laws destroyed the progress that had been made toward equal treatment of all people.

Before "Jim Crow," African Americans and Caucasians had begun to eat in the same restaurants. They rode in the same railway cars. They used the same restrooms and sat together in the same theaters. They might not have been friends, but they were not enemies.

But in 1896 the U.S. Supreme Court said it was legal to keep African Americans "separate but equal." Soon two cultures were in place. One was Caucasian. The other was African American.

African Americans could not go to "white" parks. They could not swim in "white" pools. They could not use "white" restrooms. They could not drink from "white" water fountains. They could not go to "white" schools. They could not apply for "white" jobs. They could not play on "white" sports teams. They were *segregated,* or kept apart, in nearly every way.

Because they were kept apart from Caucasian culture, African Americans developed their own culture. African American baseball teams were an important part of that culture. In some cities, the African American baseball teams were the only form of African American entertainment.

African American baseball teams continued to grow. In 1885 the first all-black professional baseball team started in New York. Other teams began to spring up so more African American athletes could play ball.

Remember Fowler, the man who invented shin guards to protect his legs? He started his own team in Michigan. He named it the Page Fence Giants. In 1897 Fowler's team won 82 games in a row! It was the best African American team in the country.

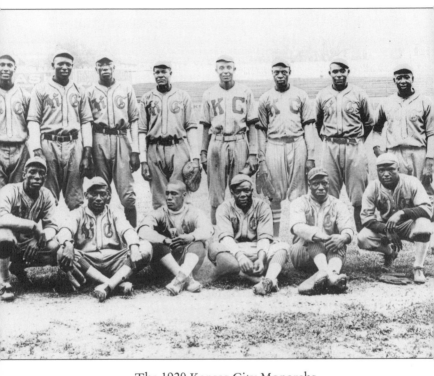

The 1920 Kansas City Monarchs,
a Negro National League team

Fowler did not have a home field for his team. The Giants played all their games away. They traveled in their own railroad car. A cook went with them. They ate their meals on the train. They slept on the train because African Americans could not stay in most hotels.

*Finding places to stay and food to eat were constant challenges for most African American teams. Sometimes they found rooming houses. Sometimes they slept in the homes of fans. When they could find no other beds, they even slept in small-town jails! And when there was no place to stop, they slept sitting up on the team bus.

It was also hard to find places to eat. Most Caucasian-owned diners would not serve African Americans. Many players brought their food with them. Canned fish was popular. It didn't taste great, but the cans kept the fish fresh. Other teams played as many as three games a day on empty stomachs. But when African American teams ran onto the field, they put the hard times aside. There, they were heroes.

Their* fans loved them! The fans knew the "scoop" on every player. Even though not every town had an African American team, fans everywhere knew what was happening in the Negro Leagues. They read about the players in the national African American weekly newspapers.

African American teams provided more than just entertainment. The players served as role models for youngsters. They also provided jobs for players, coaches, cooks, and water boys. Team owners rented local ballparks for their games.

Fans spent money on tickets—lots of tickets! The first East-West All-Star game between the best Negro League teams drew 20,000 fans. This was in 1933, during the Great Depression! By the mid-1940s, the Negro Leagues were the largest African American businesses in the country.

— Chapter 4 —

A Roster of Greats

African American teams were very popular—and very successful. They drew both African American and Caucasian fans to their games because their players were so outstanding.

For nearly 30 years, Bell was the fastest man in baseball. It is said he could run all the bases in 11 seconds flat! During some seasons, he had a .400 batting average. He hit so well and ran so fast that another player on his team made up a tall tale about him.

The player said Bell once hit a ground ball past the pitcher. Then he ran so fast that he got to second base before the ball arrived. His own grounder hit him in the leg just as he slid into second!

Gibson, Bell's teammate, played 17 years in the Negro Leagues. Catchers are often not great hitters, but Gibson was. He had a .391 lifetime batting average. It was the highest in the Negro Leagues. Gibson also hit nearly 800 home runs.

Another star player was Martín Dihigo. He first played in 1923 on a team called the Cuban Stars. His Cuban fans called him "the Master." No wonder! He may have been the best all-around player of all time.

Dihigo played all nine positions. He was an outstanding pitcher and batter. He won three Negro National League home run crowns and tied with Gibson for a fourth.

Dihigo also played baseball in Mexico. Fans there loved him too. He is the only player ever elected to the Baseball Hall of Fame in three countries—Cuba, Mexico, and the United States.

One of the most popular players of all time was Paige. He started playing in the 1920s. Paige was a great pitcher. He seemed to have a hundred ways to throw the ball.

Some of his pitches, such as his "hesitation ball," were funny. Paige had long, spiderlike legs and an expressive face. He would wind up before throwing the ball. Then he would stop and make faces at the fans. They loved his clowning as well as his pitching. Paige had a long career. He played on many teams. He always drew a big crowd.

Leroy "Satchel" Paige (#29) winds up on
the mound to throw a pitch

Even the "white" newspapers covered Paige. They did not write about African American sports often. But Paige gave good interviews. He always had something funny to say. One of his sayings was, "Don't look back. Something may be gaining on you."[1] Reporters praised Paige's talent. They called him "the pitcher's pitcher." Stories about him drew Caucasian fans to games.

Paige and other stars made African American baseball popular. African American owners were determined to keep ownership of those teams in African American hands. In 1920 Rube Foster of the Chicago Giants called a meeting with other team owners. Foster wanted to keep Negro League teams under the control of African Americans.

So Foster and seven others formed the Negro National League (NNL). Foster was elected president of the league. *He became known as "the father of black baseball." He and the other owners set game schedules. They made rules about treating players fairly. And they worked out ways to draw more fans.

The first NNL teams were in the Midwest. Some of the teams were the Detroit Stars, the Kansas City Monarchs, the St. Louis Giants, and the Cuban Stars.

Other leagues formed in the East and the South. Caucasian businessmen formed the Eastern Colored League. The Caucasian-owned league had six teams. They competed with one another and with NNL teams.

Like other Negro League teams, they traveled all over the country. Over the years, several dozen teams played in the Negro Leagues.

Some states had only one team. The only team in Arkansas was the Little Rock Black* Travelers. Other states had many teams. Ohio had 18!

Chapter 5

Equals on the Field

Major league Caucasian teams were still not signing African American players. But each year they played against them in *barnstorming*, or exhibition, games. African American teams had played each other for years in these traveling competitions.

When major league teams got into the act during the 1930s and 1940s, all-star teams of major leaguers traveled the country. They played against the best African American teams. Why? The reason was simple. It was a way to make money during the off-season.

African American players loved to play against Caucasian teams. Each player made around 200 to 250 dollars per game. This was much less than the Caucasian players made. But it was a whole month's pay in the Negro Leagues! The games also made the African American players proud. The African American team beat the Caucasian team 60 percent of the time!

The best Caucasian pitchers often lost to African American teams. Jay "Dizzy" Dean once lost four of six games to Paige. Dean told him, "You're a better pitcher than I ever hope to be, Satchel."[2]

Matchups against Paige always pulled in fans of both races. He was paid very well and put on quite a show. He clearly had a great time doing it.

[2] Text copyright © 1962 by David Lipman from the book MAYBE I'LL PITCH FOREVER published by The Curtis Publishing Company. Reprinted by permission of McIntosh and Otis, Inc.

"It got so I could nip frosting off a cake with my fastball," Paige boasted. "My philosophy is simple. Keep the ball away from the bat."[3]

The fans ate it up. They loved it when the Satchel Paige All-Stars went up against Bob Feller's All-Stars. Feller, a major league pitcher, called Paige "the best pitcher I ever saw."

The African American all-star teams got a lot of respect. Still, they had to find ways to keep the crowds coming back. The teams often used stunts to draw fans. Sometimes they warmed up by playing blindfolded. Sometimes they played "ghost ball," going through the motions without a ball. The players were funny!

[3] Text copyright © 1962 by David Lipman from the book MAYBE I'LL PITCH FOREVER published by The Curtis Publishing Company. Reprinted by permission of McIntosh and Otis, Inc.

Special guests drew in fans too. Olympic champion Jesse Owens sprinted. Female golfer Babe Didrickson pitched.

In 1930, team owner J. L. Wilkinson had a bright idea—lights! He rigged portable outdoor lights for his team, the Kansas City Monarchs. This made it possible for them to play at night. Negro League teams were always looking for ways to make money. Night games were another way to bring in fans. Major league teams did not use lights until 1935.

To make a living, African American players had to play year-round. First they played their regular season. Then they barnstormed. When it got cold, they went south of the U.S. border to play.

*Some played in Mexico. Some played in Cuba. Others went to Venezuela or Puerto Rico to play. The Spanish-speaking baseball fans loved the players.

Owners of these teams paid well. So Caucasian major league players played there too. Caucasians and African Americans played with teammates who were from Cuba and Mexico.

Players of all races got to know one another by playing on the same teams. Most players respected each other. Some became friends. Many Caucasian players said baseball back home was not fair to African American players.

Some African American players did not go back to the United States. The money was better elsewhere. The climate was sunny. And best of all, fans of all races respected them.

Willie Wells, who played for the Newark Eagles, chose to stay* in Mexico. "Not only do I make more money, I live like a king . . . ," he said. "I was branded a Negro in the United States and had to act accordingly. . . . Well, here in Mexico, I am a man. I can go as far in baseball as I am capable of going."[4]

Wells did not make the common choice. Usually players chose to go home. Some could not stand the intense heat. Many did not speak Spanish. Their roots were in the United States. They came back, hoping conditions would change. Thanks to a man named Branch Rickey, they finally did.

[4] Excerpt from THE STORY OF NEGRO LEAGUE BASEBALL by William Brashler. Copyright © 1994 by William Brashler. Reprinted by permission of Houghton Mifflin Company. All rights reserved.

Chapter 6

A Beginning and an End

Segregation was not the only thing keeping African American players out of the major leagues. Money was another. Owners of Caucasian ball fields made huge sums renting out their fields to African American teams. It was to their advantage to keep the Negro Leagues separate.

The idea that an African American player would bring in money was the argument Rickey used when he hired Robinson. In 1942, when Rickey became general manager of the Brooklyn Dodgers, he soon saw that the team didn't make much money.

Rickey felt segregation was morally wrong. Yet he knew just doing the right thing would not sell Robinson to Dodgers fans. Boosting the team's ticket sales and win record would. He began planning how to integrate the team.

Rickey did not talk about fair treatment for African American players. He knew this would anger fans who believed in segregation. Still, he wanted to do the right thing. Something that had happened years before had opened his eyes.

In 1904 Rickey had been a baseball coach at an Ohio college. The team rode the bus to an away game. When an African American player named Charlie Thomas was turned away from the team's hotel, Rickey talked the desk clerk into letting Thomas stay in his room.

Thomas was hurt by what had happened. He cried and rubbed his skin. "If only I could rub it off!" he said.

Rickey promised himself that someday he would correct the situation. "The scene haunted me for years," Rickey said, "and I vowed I would do whatever I could to see that other Americans did not have to face the bitter humiliation that was heaped upon Charlie Thomas."

Three years after he joined the Dodgers, Rickey broke the "color barrier" that shut out African American players. He scouted the Negro Leagues for just the right player. The man had to be a great athlete. He also had to be tough. He had to be able to handle insults.

Robinson was the man for the job. He had played four sports in college. He had been in the army. Then he had played for a leading Negro League team.

Robinson told Rickey he could handle whatever came his way. In 1946 he played for a year on the Dodger's farm team. Then, in 1947, he put on the Dodger uniform and took his place at first base.

It was hard. People shouted insults. They called Robinson names. They said they would kill him. Pitchers threw balls at his head. Players spiked him when they slid into first base.

Branch Rickey picked Jackie Robinson to
break the color barrier in the major leagues

Through it all, Robinson kept his cool. He did not fall to the level of some fans and players. He did not call anyone names. He let his talent speak for him. In 1947 he helped his team win the National League pennant. He was named Rookie of the Year.

In 1949 Robinson was named the league's Most Valuable Player. His batting average was .342. He stole 37 bases. He batted in 124 runs. During his ten years with the Dodgers, they played in six World Series.

Robinson retired in 1957. He was still at the top of his game. After retiring from baseball he had a long business career. He also worked in the civil rights movement.

Robinson was the first of many African American players to play in the major leagues. In 1946 the Dodgers hired two more—Don Newcombe and Roy Campanella. Campanella was voted the league's Most Valuable Player three times. Newcombe, a pitcher, was named Rookie of the Year.

Other teams saw the money the Dodgers were making. The skills of their African American players drew big crowds.

These teams followed the Dodgers' lead. Baseball began to hire young Negro League players. It was too late for those players who had been the backbone of the league. Bell, Gibson, and many others were now too old. The teams wanted younger players.

After a home run, two Caucasian teammates shake hands
with Roy Campanella as he crosses home plate

*Paige was the exception. He was about 40 years old in 1948 when Cleveland signed him. He pitched his last major league game in 1965. He was around 57 years old!

Major league teams had the cash to bring the best African American players to the major leagues. Fans wanted to watch the top players. The Negro Leagues could not afford the top players, so fewer and fewer fans came to their games. When they started, the Negro Leagues gave African American players a place to play baseball. After the players were accepted in the major leagues, the Negro Leagues folded.

The Negro Leagues were an important part of baseball history. They showed that African American players were as good as Caucasian players and that they deserved to play in* the same league. Once there were two sets of leagues—one African American and one Caucasian. By 1960 there was no reason for more than one.